First published in the UK by HarperCollins Children's Books in 2009
1 3 5 7 9 10 8 6 4 2
ISBN: 978-0-00-731497-3
A CIP Catalogue record for this title is available from the British Library.
No part of this publication may be reproduced, stored in a retrieval system or transmitted in any form or
by any means, electronic, mechanical, photocopying, recording or otherwise, without the prior permission of
HarperCollins Publishers Ltd, 77-85 Fulham Palace Road, Hammersmith, London W6 8JB

www.harpercollins.co.uk

The Me to You oval, Tatty Teddy signature and Bear logo are all registered
Trade Marks of Carte Blanche Greetings Ltd. © Carte Blanche Greetings Ltd
® PO Box 500, Chichester, PO20 2XZ, UK

www.carteblanchegreetings.com

Printed and bound in Italy by L.E.G.O. Spa

Wonderful Wife

To have a Wife
is to have a
friend forever

It's easy to love
the love of your life

A Wife makes

A HOUSE A HOME

To share your life
with someone
is wonderful

The best thing about
being married is sharing
my life with you

A Wife should be
loved and adored...
forever

The most special friend
a man will ever have
is his Wife

A loving Wife is
always there for you

A Wife is someone
you create
memories with

A Wife can always
be relied upon

I appreciate you
in so many ways

I'm so lucky to
SHARE my life
with you